The Economic Consequences of Political Independence

The Case of Bermuda

The Economic Consequences of Political Independence

The Case of Bermuda

James C.W. Ahiakpor

The Fraser Institute
Vancouver, British Columbia, Canada

Canadian Cataloguing in Publication Data

Ahiakpor, James.
The economic consequences of political independence

Includes bibliographical references.
ISBN 0-88975-123-4

1. Bermuda Islands - Economic policy.
2. Bermuda Islands - Economic conditions.
3. Bermuda Islands - Politics and government.
I. Fraser Institute (Vancouver, B.C.).
II. Title.

HC592.5.A54 1989   330.97299   C89-091645-4

Printed in Canada.

Contents

List of Tables

Table

Foreword

Freedom and Economic Development

For three years the Fraser Institute has conducted a project examining the relationship between economic development and civil, political, and economic freedoms. The purpose of the project is ultimately to construct a global index of economic freedom and thereby to facilitate such an examination. Such an index could also be used in analysis to predict the economic consequence of changes in the level of economic freedom in different countries.

In the course of this research two very interesting political entities have come to the attention of researchers. Both are British colonies, both have achieved extraordinary economic success by comparison with other countries having similar opportunities, and neither has the true political independence and political autonomy which is a characteristic of independent sovereign nation states. The two countries are Hong Kong and Bermuda. Both, for different reasons, are considering the potential effects of a separation in their relationship with Great Britain. In the case of Hong Kong it is because of the running out in 1997 of the agreement between Britain and China regarding British tenure at Hong Kong Island. In the case of Bermuda, the pressure is emerging from within Bermuda itself and is a reverberation of the kind of independence wave which swept the British Empire following the Second World War.

In this book Professor James Ahiakpor, a participant in the Fraser Institute Rating Economic Freedom project, courageously undertakes an examination of the consequences for Bermuda should independence form a part of the island country's future. I'm sure that those who are concerned about the future of Bermuda will find his analysis both interesting and useful. Some will be surprised by the views which Professor Ahiakpor expresses, but not by the engaging way in which he expresses them.

For its part, the Fraser Institute has been pleased to sponsor Professor Ahiakpor's research and to publish it for the wider consideration of those concerned about the relationship between political, economic, and civil freedoms, and in particular those who are interested in the future of Bermuda. The views expressed by Professor Ahiakpor have been arrived at independently, however, and do not necessarily reflect the views of the members or the Trustees of the Fraser Institute.

Michael A. Walker
October 20, 1989

Preface

Being politically free is a cherished goal of many people. Pursuit of that goal has led to wars of political independence or liberation being fought over the ages. But in the case of Bermuda, most people do not feel that being under the (indirect) rule of the British Crown amounts to a loss of their political freedom in any meaningful way. Indeed, the people of Bermuda, through their parliament, have virtually total control over all facets of their lives except in matters of external representation and national security.

In spite of Britain's willingness to grant this island country political independence upon request, that request has yet to be presented, although the independence question has been debated actively since 1977. Indeed, most Bermudians rather see political independence as incurring the costs of external representation and national defence without tangible benefits in return. The debate over the desirability of political independence still continues, even if muted because of the Premier's decision in September 1988 to suspend active consideration of it.

I have tried to examine arguments on both sides of the issue in an attempt to assess the "economic" consequences of political independence. I have not limited my definition of "economic" to cash or financial considerations only. Rather, my definition follows the classical tradition (the method of Adam Smith, David Ricardo, John Stuart Mill, and Alfred Marshall) which entails examination of all kinds of choices that may affect an individual's state of well-being. Marshall (1964, Book 1, chapter 2) explains that "the side of life with which economics is specially concerned is that in which man's conduct is most deliberate, and in which he most often reckons up the advantages and disadvantages of any particular action before he enters on it." He adds, "though it is true that 'money' or 'general purchasing power' or 'command over material wealth,' is the centre around which economic science clusters; this is so, not because money or material wealth is regarded as the main aim for the study of the economist, but because in this world of ours it is the one convenient means of measuring human motive on a large scale" (p. 18). In other words, the analytical tools of economics can be applied to the study of choices which do not involve cash calculations. This I attempt to do in this study. Therefore, those looking mainly for some 'hard' dollar values as the consequences of political independence may be disappointed with my analysis. But the study is not without numbers either.

In the main, examination of the issues leads me to conclude that both sides to the independence debate have bits of exaggeration in their claims. It does not seem plausible that political independence would ruin Bermuda's potential for continued economic success. The costs of independence, however inaccurately they may have been estimated, also do not appear beyond the means of Bermudians. On the other hand, whatever benefits there might be from becoming politically independent do not now seem to be worth the costs. These benefits include formulation of foreign policy, internal control of the security forces, and fostering a greater sense of Bermudianness—the most doubtful of all the expected benefits. However, the benefit/cost calculations may change in the future, depending upon how Bermudians perceive their relations with the British Crown.

I come to these conclusions in full recognition of the fact that it would be hard for a foreigner to feel fully what natives of another country feel. But the conclusions are based on both the views (or revealed preferences) of Bermudians and an examination of comparable evidence elsewhere. Indeed, it has been much of a personal education for me to undertake this study. My own feeling upon being given the assignment was that of extreme surprise that a people—predominantly Black at that!—would have hesitations about obtaining political independence from Britain. But I have since come to appreciate the logic of their preference.

I do not expect everyone actively concerned with or engaged in the independence debate to find all aspects of my analysis satisfactory. Some readers may find my discussions at places not detailed enough; indeed each of the issues discussed in the various chapters could be dealt with extensively on its own. I chose my present approach in order (I hope) not to stray much from the main focus, the immediate debate on independence for Bermuda.

There are those who would consider the independence question beyond benefit/cost calculations. To them, political independence is a matter of birthright. In the words of Lester Bird (Antigua and Barbuda 1979), "to be free is our right, to be independent is our absolute right." But not even they would deny that in the act of making any choice something else is always given up, and it is legitimate for people to differ on the assessment of the values traded in the process. If this study helps to clarify some of the issues that require further examination in deciding the independence question, I would consider its purpose to have been served.

Acknowledgements

In the course of this study (or my education), I have benefited from the kind assistance of several people, for which I am very grateful. I thank in particular, John Scrymgeour, Don Mason, and Derek and Marie Joell for helping me to obtain research materials and arranging interviews with several knowledgeable people in Bermuda. For sparing time to discuss with me aspects of life in Bermuda (society and economy) related to the research, I thank in particular David Allen, Eugene Blakeney, Walter Brangman, Kirk Cooper, Gilbert Darrell, Joe Johnson, John Ken, Allan Marshall, Nellie Musson, Thomas Nisbett, Cyril Packwood, Calvin Smith, Luelle Todd, Jim Turnbull, Nick Weinreb, Jim Woolridge, and Bill Zuill. Most of these interviews were conducted between August 27 and September 3, 1988, when I visited Bermuda. Comments, criticisms, and suggestions from Don Mason, Michael Walker, and two anonymous readers of an earlier draft were also helpful in shaping the final form of the manuscript. Finally, I thank Michael Walker, Executive Director of the Fraser Institute, for the invitation and subsequent support to do the study. Responsibility for the views expressed here rests with me.

James C.W. Ahiakpor

About the Author

Born in Ghana, James Ahiakpor earned his B.Sc. (Economics) and M.Sc. (Economics) from the University of Ghana, Legon. He taught economics at that university from 1973 to 1976. He came to Canada in 1976 and obtained an M.A. in economics from the University of British Columbia and a Ph.D. from the University of Toronto where he specialized in monetary theory and development economics. A professor of economics at Saint Mary's University since 1981, James Ahiakpor teaches economic theory, development economics, the history of economic thought, and money and banking. He has published widely in such periodicals as the *Journal of Development Economics, Economic Development and Cultural Change, History of Political Economy, International Organization, Southern Economic Journal,* and the *Canadian Journal of African Studies.* He is also a contributing author to the Fraser Institute's 1986 book, *Reaction: The New Combines Investigation Act.* Dr. Ahiakpor is currently completing a book on multinationals and economic development.

Chapter One

Political Independence and Economic Performance

The performance of an economy is fundamentally tied to politics because political control is often the first step in determining economic policy. In another sense, political conflicts may be understood as attempts by people to control the environment in which they create and spend their wealth. Those who hold political power may determine the amount and extent of taxation, regulation of business enterprises, commerce (both domestic and foreign), and the rights of individuals to own and control property. For a nation, the ability to exercise political control without seeking the approval of an external power may thus be a freedom of fundamental importance.

History illustrates the struggles for political freedom undertaken to control a people's economic destiny. For example, the American war of independence from England was fought mainly in order to wrest political control from the British Crown so as to determine the extent of taxation and the uses of tax revenue in the then colony. In modern times, wars of independence have been fought in the Third World. Their leaders believed that the colonial masters had held back economic development to keep them as dependent purchasers of manufactures while the natural resources of colonial countries were extracted with little or no benefits to the colonial peoples. This thinking was very much present in arguments by Mahatma Gandhi of India in his campaign for that country's independence. He even persuaded thousands of people to burn their imported clothes. The intent was to deny British textile mills an export market, although that action probably hurt the people of India more than it affected the British.

Similarly, Kwame Nkrumah of Ghana summarized his view of colonialism as "the policy by which a foreign power binds territories to herself by political ties with the primary object of promoting her own economic advantage" (Nkrumah 1959, p. v). Nkrumah (1963, p. 21) based his views partly on arguments by two French officials who claimed that "colonies are for rich countries one of the most lucrative methods of investing capital…outlets for [their] manufacture" (Jules Ferry, Premier of France, 1885), and "the people who set out to seize colonies in distant lands were thinking primarily of themselves, and

2

were working for their own profits, and conquering for their own power" (Albert Sarraut, French Colonial Secretary of State, 1923). Nkrumah also was much influenced by black movements in the U.S. during the late 1930s and early 1940s, including the views of Marcus Garvey. He engaged in a relentless struggle to free the Gold Coast (Ghana) of colonial rule.

Wars of secession have been fought in order to gain greater political control by a people who felt exploited by their central government. For example, the war between Bangladesh, formerly East Pakistan, and West Pakistan (now Pakistan) in the early 1970s was mainly over the right of the former to control its economic destiny. The relative poverty of Bangladesh was believed to have been due to the neglect it suffered from the central government controlled by West Pakistan.

The war between Eastern Nigeria, which sought to declare an independent state of Biafra in the late 1960s, was similarly motivated. Its aim was to end Northern control over political power so that the Easterners could determine their own economic survival. Kwame Nkrumah probably put the argument for political independence most succinctly thus:

seek ye first the political kingdom and all others shall be added on to you.

As will become evident below, these arguments for political independence do not apply to Bermuda's circumstances today. It may surprise many to find a colony in which a significant majority of people do not want political independence, as is the case in Bermuda. According to an opinion poll conducted by the *Royal Gazette* and published in June 1988, as much as 80 percent of respondents opposed independence from Britain. The scientifically conducted random poll (estimated to be accurate to within plus or minus five percentage points) involved 500 people, 57 percent of whom were black, 39 percent white, and 4 percent who classified themselves as "other"; 16 percent of the sample were born outside Bermuda. (See *The Royal Gazette*, 15 June 1988.)

The other notable aspect of this stance of Bermudians is that opposition to political independence has increased since polls started being taken on the issue in 1977. In that year the level of opposition was 55 percent. It increased to 66 percent in 1982. And 87 percent of those polled in 1988 claimed they did not have enough information about the pros and cons of becoming politically independent. However, such a claim likely represents not so much a lack of adequate information for a people as literate, travelled, and wealthy as Bermudians, but a fundamental lack of interest in political independence.

The inclination of most Bermudians against political independence can be explained. Among the reasons often given are:

(a) Bermuda is already a self-governing country with its own freely elected

4

parliament and a Governor who does not act without first consulting with the Premier and two or three members of his cabinet;

(b) Under the present constitutional arrangement, Britain assumes responsibility for the Island's foreign policy, including external representation (thus the Bermudian passport carries easy recognition), and Britain provides a security (national defence) umbrella for the colony;

(c) The present constitutional arrangement also provides a sense of social and political stability: people, particularly, foreigners doing business in the colony, may feel they have ultimate redress from Great Britain should they be aggrieved by some government action;

(d) Because of their relatively high per capita income, higher than those of the U.S., Britain, and Canada (see table 1), they fear a possible economic deterioration following the attainment of political independence, just as has happened in some Caribbean, African, and Asian countries since the Second World War.

Table 1

Per Capita National Incomes: Bermuda, Britain, Canada, and the United States (US$)

	1980	1983	1985
Bermuda	n.a.*	14,722	16,816
	(10,700)	(14,393)	(16,265)
Britain	9,809	7,808	9,056
	(9,818)	(7,746)	(8,969)
Canada	10,552	12,716	13,024
	(10,826)	(13,095)	(13,436)
United States	11,996	14,521	16,709
	(11,787)	(14,308)	(16,537)

Note: Values for countries other than Bermuda were calculated from data reported in *International Financial Statistics* (1987). Values for Bermuda are based on tables 8.1 and 8.4 in *Bermuda Digest of Statistics* (1987). Values in brackets are gross domestic product per capita in current prices.

*n.a. = not available

Many Bermudians feel they have "the best of both worlds"—economic prosperity and political stability. "Why fix that which is not broken?," many ask.

Besides the fear of political instability that might follow independence, many worry about the direct costs of independence. These include the cost of increasing the national defence force and the police service, the cost of national representation abroad, including the country's membership in some world organizations such as the United Nations and its specialized agencies, the World Bank and the International Monetary Fund. Without any significant expected benefits from full political independence, many see it mainly as incurring avoidable costs.

There is substantial validity to most of the above fears or arguments. But several of them also entail exaggerations or only partial truth. For example, some have claimed that the additional cost of independence could amount to $5,000 per capita. Defence costs alone would increase to $12 million (or about $207 per capita). Others project substantial job losses after independence. But if such were the case, many Third World countries, including several in the Caribbean, would have gone bankrupt by now after having attained political independence. Few of them have per capita national incomes anywhere near the costs of independence claimed for Bermuda.

To enable a more informed choice to be made, these arguments need careful examination. This study attempts such an examination. I do not come up with "hard" numbers for the cost of political independence for Bermuda, but from examination of the economic and political performance of many Third World countries following their independence and the recent history of Bermuda, I find little basis for the fear of significant, adverse economic consequences of political independence.

On the other hand, there now seems to be little to gain from independence. Thus, unless political and social circumstances change in Bermuda, a benefit/cost calculation of political independence would appear negative for most people, hence collectively as well.

Chapter Two

The Logic of Political Independence for Bermuda

The question of political independence for a country follows logically from its history. Many of those who raise the issue and are eager for Bermuda to attain constitutional independence from Britain also appear to take this view. Thus, casting the independence question in a historical context may aid in understanding the choice problem facing Bermudians.

Early Beginnings

Settlement of the islands that constitute Bermuda is dated from July 1609 when the surviving crew of a British vessel, the *Sea Venture,* heading for Virginia was wrecked

9

on the coral reefs off the coast of Bermuda. Although the island was originally discovered in 1511 by a Spanish sea captain, Juan de Bermudez, from whose name Bermuda is derived, the crew of the shipwreck found no permanent settlement when they arrived. The attractiveness of the place led them to seek a charter from the King of England to establish a permanent settlement there. The charter, granted to the Somers Island Company (1612), provided British settlers with a legal claim to the island, a claim that could be enforced by the authority of the British Crown.

Until the British Crown took direct control in governing the island in 1684, Bermuda was a private company-owned settlement. Civil life was modelled along British parliamentary tradition, the island having established its own parliament in 1620, making Bermuda the third country after Britain and Iceland to practise parliamentary rule. Other private companies, besides the Somers Island (or the Bermuda) Company also operated in different parts of the island. These companies constituted private monopolies with their own spheres of influence in parts of Bermuda.

From this tradition of British settlement, request for political independence may be an attempt by descendants of British settlers to rid themselves of the legal authority the British Crown has over their affairs through the charters under which original settlement was protected. However, the most ardent seekers of political independence are not the descendants of British settlers of the island, but blacks. Some of them claim that political independence derives logically from their emancipation from slavery.

Blacks originally were imported into Bermuda by British settlers as skilled labour in the early 17th century. Official accounts state that black slaves were first brought from the Caribbean Islands in 1616 to dive for pearls or for their agricultural skills. Some were raided off slave ships headed for the Americas, while others went to Bermuda as indentured workers.

Some authors dispute the claim that blacks first went to Bermuda as slaves. Packwood (1975, p. 2) argues that during the first decade of the island's settlement blacks and Indians were imported as indentured workers. Smith (1976, pp. 12-13) makes the same argument. However, both agree that blacks were predominantly slaves during the early period of Bermuda's history.

Financial indebtedness of many indentured black workers also led them to convert to slavery. They substituted loss of property rights in themselves for the burden of being financially in debt. Others went into slavery not of their own volition but of that of their parents. There are stories of children, especially daughters, being given away to wealthy white Bermudians by their aging parents (e.g. Packwood 1975, p. 4). The declared intent of such an act was to ensure a life of material security for the child. They apparently did not consider that giving their children away was a diminution of their humanity or deprivation of freedom in any meaningful way.

Blacks constituted the main source of labour for the island's economy. They worked on the land, growing tobacco, potatoes, sugar-cane, rice, indigo, bananas, and other crops. Fishing, whaling, and shipbuilding were other important early industries in which slave labour was employed by white settlers of Bermuda and their descendants.

Over time the population of Bermuda evolved from being predominantly white with a few skilled free black workers and slaves to that of a substantially mixed group. By 1691 the population of whites was estimated at 4,331, that of slaves at 1,917. But before emancipation in 1834 the black population exceeded the white. In 1822 the number of whites was estimated at 4,648, free blacks at 722, and slaves at 5,242 (Packwood 1975, pp. 74, 75). Blacks have formed the majority of Bermuda's population ever since despite several attempts to restrict their number, and they now constitute about 60 percent of Bermuda's population.

Until the late 1960s the economic, legal, and political status of Bermudian blacks evolved slowly following the official Act of Emancipation in 1834. Although the property right of self was restored by the official abolition of slavery, the material poverty of many freed slaves was such that they depended very much for their survival on the pleasures of whites and former slave masters who owned virtually all non-human wealth or physical property of economic significance. Freed slaves could rent their human capital or skills to white employers in exchange for cash income. However, whites owned much of the material wealth and also enjoyed monopoly rights over the legal instruments of power.

In contrast with other former slave economies based mainly on sugar plantations, the condition of blacks in Bermuda was much better. The diversified economy provided them with opportunities to acquire skills with which they were able to share better in the country's economic fortunes, even if not as equals with whites. (For details see Packwood 1975, Smith 1976, and Musson 1979.)

Thus, until the middle 1960s, administration of the island rested in the hands of people (whites) of material wealth. It was from among them that legislators were elected. Wealth requirements virtually assured exclusion of blacks from participation in civic elections and thus limited their ability to influence laws to their own advantage. It is this climate of legal and economic control by the materially wealthy class of Bermudians that is sometimes referred to as the "rule of forty thieves."

The Modern Era

Blacks in Bermuda, as they have done in other parts of the world, constantly sought to change the legal, political, and economic institutions to improve their lives and fortunes. However, such avenues were often blocked by whites who had control over the legal and political instruments of power. The drive for constitutional change, and perhaps the opposition to it on the part of whites, may have been influenced by the attainment of political independence for blacks in Africa (led south of the Sahara by Ghana in 1957) and later by others in the Caribbean. Black movements in the United States also may have provided additional encouragement to blacks in Bermuda to seek equality of rights in the legal and political spheres of life. The earlier influence of Marcus Garvey on the island had been almost eliminated through official harassment of his followers in the late 1930s. (See, for example, Musson 1979, chapter 13.)

Blacks sought desegregation of movie theatres in Bermuda through their 1959 boycott (led by Dr. Stanley Ratteray, Mr. Kingsley Tweed, and others). As a result, blacks no longer were confined to only the lower sitting area of theatres. Similarly, agitation in 1960 against the property requirements for eligibility to vote by the Committee for Universal Adult Suffrage culminated in the vote being given to all Bermudians over the age of 25 in 1963. However, those who owned property of significance, typically beyond the means of most blacks, retained the privilege of a second vote.

Articulation of the aspirations of blacks for legal and political equality in Bermuda initially took the form of action groups such as the Theatre Boycott movement and the Committee for Universal Adult Suffrage. Such movements received some support from white Bermudians as well. But by 1963 a political party emerged dedicated to promoting the cause of blacks and labour, the Progressive Labour Party (PLP) led by Mrs. Lois Browne-Evans. Six of its candidates were elected in 1963 into a 36-member legislature during the first general election in which the franchise was granted to all Bermudians aged 25 years and over.

The PLP's success under universal adult suffrage led to the coalition of 24 other elected like-minded members of the legislature, both black and white, under the leadership of Sir Henry Tucker to form the United Bermuda Party (UBP) in 1964. Because of their number in the legislature, the UBP immediately became the governing party in Bermuda. The inclusion of a significant number of blacks among important positions in the UBP also diffused what could have been the basis of future political power for the PLP—the redress of legal and political inequalities for blacks in Bermuda. Thus the UBP emphasizes integration of the races in a common search for material and social progress for Bermudians. On the other hand, the PLP and its splinter party, the National Liberal Party of Bermuda

(NLP), point to economic and social inequalities among Bermudians, mainly on the basis of race, and the need for blacks to mobilize their political power to redress them.

The Logic of Political Independence

Political independence means different things to different people in Bermuda, black or white. To some blacks, especially those affiliated with the PLP and NLP, independence represents the ultimate liberation from a status of subservience to the white population. They regard the island as dominated in the spheres of economics and political administration by whites and foreigners from England. Some also believe present arrangements to restrict the inflow of immigrants have been implemented mainly to restrain the growth of the black population. (Indeed, the share of blacks in the population has declined slightly since 1960 from about 63 percent to the present 60 percent.) They think there is an attempt to increase the white population, particularly skilled and managerial personnel from Britain. Political independence, which in their view would force all residents to choose between being Bermudians or other nationalities, would ensure that only those who feel strongly about being Bermudians settle on the island. These blacks consider others of their kind who support the UBP as lacking the right social (racial) consciousness because of affluence or their anticipation of economic prosperity in the future.

On the other hand, many blacks do not now see the need for political independence in order to enhance their material and social well-being. They are invariably supporters of the UBP, although not all supporters of the other parties want political independence. (There are UBP members who support the move for Bermuda's political independence, including Premier John Swan, who is black.) They want to see Bermuda run by a mixture of blacks and whites who think of Bermuda as a nation first. Though usually more affluent than most other blacks, these supporters of the UBP deny that their political support has been bought by the white business class. Rather, they believe their success has been earned through hard work and that it is possible for others to improve their lot that way.

To these blacks there is little to become independent of since Bermudians have, for all practical purposes, been their own masters since the 1970s, being able to enact legislation and run the country under a Governor who hardly acts without consultation with the Premier and an advisory council composed of Bermudians. Until they see significant positive contributions to their lives from political independence, they are content with the present constitutional arrangement.

On the part of most whites, the present constitutional status of Bermuda is conducive to their well-being as well as that of other Bermudians. Unlike the whites in Southern Rhodesia led by Ian Smith who unilaterally declared independence from Britain in 1965, few think they need political independence to organize Bermudian society in a form that would assure continuity of their economic prosperity. Many fear a possible deterioration in economic conditions as well as in political administration similar to the experience of several former British colonies following independence. Frequent coups, rule by tyrants who deny civil liberties to most of the population, rampant corruption, and civil wars have plagued many of these countries.

Typically, deterioration in political administration was quickly followed by economic collapse. For a detailed discussion of these experiences in Africa between 1960 and 1985, see Duignan and Jackson (1986).

Many whites focus on the financial costs of independence in terms of greater expenditures on external defence, foreign representation, and internal security. These costs are now borne mainly by Britain and partly by the U.S. and Canada in exchange for the operation of military bases on the island.

Although majority opinion is against Bermuda becoming independent soon, it does not mean most Bermudians agree with the fears of economic collapse. Examination of the record of recently independent nations in the next chapter confirms the fact that economic and political disasters are not the necessary outcomes of political independence, even in Africa. But neither does the record show political independence to be a necessary requirement for economic prosperity, a fact to which Bermuda's own economic history or Hong Kong's testifies.

Chapter Three

*The Development Record of Recently
Independent Countries*

As already noted, one of the important issues in the
debate over the desirability of seeking political
independence for Bermuda is whether it might lead to the
country's impressive record of economic development over
the decades being reversed. This concern is real. Many
countries that became independent after the Second World
War have failed to achieve the kind of economic
development their political leaders led them to believe
would be forthcoming.

One could dismiss this concern out of hand with the
argument that whatever happened to other countries upon
becoming politically independent need not happen to

Bermuda. Indeed, some Bermudians react with resentment to the warning that several recently independent countries have retrogressed in their development efforts. They point out that Bermudians are capable of learning from the failures of other countries. Moreover, they argue, Bermuda is already a developed country, and independence wouldn't cause a major deterioration of the social, political, and economic institutions that have sustained its development over the decades.

Finally, some Bermudians wonder if the warning might be racially motivated, especially since several of the economic and political failures are cited from Africa and some predominantly black Caribbean nations.

Whatever the merits of such reactions, it may still enlighten the decision-making process for Bermudians to examine more dispassionately the development record of recently independent countries. Indeed, the evidence is quite instructive.

On the whole, the development record of Third World countries since the Second World War is a mixture of successes and failures. The cases of failure are dominant among low-income countries. Indeed, 12 out of 31 countries designated as low-income economies by the World Bank, and for which data were available, experienced an actual decline in per capita income between 1965 and 1986 (see table 2). These countries are all in black Africa, including such natural resource rich countries

Table 2

Low-Income Countries with Negative Average Annual
Per Capita Income Growth, 1965 to 1986

	Per Capita GNP 1980	Per Capita GNP 1986	Percentage Growth 1965 to 1986
Zaire	220	160	-2.2
Madagascar	350	230	-1.7
Uganda	236	230	-2.6
Tanzania	280	250	-0.3
Niger	330	260	-2.2
Somalia	n.a.*	280	-0.3
Central African Republic	300	290	-0.6
Zambia	560	300	-1.7
Sudan	410	320	-0.2
Ghana	420	390	-1.7
Mauritania	440	420	-0.3
Senegal	450	420	-0.6

Source: World Bank (1982, p. 110 and 1988, p. 222). Per capita national income (GNP) values for 1980 are estimated in average 1978-80 U.S. dollars while those for 1986 are in constant 1980 dollars.

*n.a. = not available

as Ghana, Zambia, Zaire, and Uganda. According to 1988
World Bank estimates, the average annual growth rates of
per capita income measured in constant 1980 (US) dollars
between 1965 and 1986 were -1.7 percent (Ghana and
Zambia), -2.2 percent (Zaire), and -2.6 percent (Uganda).
But these are all countries that experienced modest to good
economic growth prior to and soon after political
independence.

Indeed, the poor growth performance of some countries
has led to their being reclassified from the ranks of
middle-income countries since 1976 to that of low-income
countries in 1986. They include Togo, the Sudan, Senegal,
Zambia, and Ghana. The degree of relative poverty that has
occurred in these countries may also be illustrated by how
much closer their per capita incomes have gotten to that of
the poorest country in the world. Ghana moved from being
ranked 55th on the World Bank's poverty scale in 1976 to
being 30th in 1986; Zambia, from 48th to 24th; Senegal,
from 46th to 33rd; the Sudan, from 39th to 26th; Togo,
from 35th to 15th; and Uganda, from 33rd to 12th. (Lower
ranks indicate greater relative poverty.) Many, including
some in these countries, have concluded that political
independence has been more of a curse than a blessing for
them.

However, several other low-income countries have
experienced positive economic growth over the period,
both in Africa and elsewhere. Significant among these are
Sri Lanka (2.9 percent), China (5.1 percent), and Lesotho

in Southern Africa (5.6 percent). Thus, for low-income countries as a whole, economic growth has been positive since the Second World War. Between 1965 and 1986 the average annual growth rate of per capita income for the group was 3.1 percent, although excluding China and India the growth rate was only 0.5 percent.

The poor growth record of low-income countries as a whole since 1965 reflects mostly the bad economic policy choices made by their governments. Significant among them were increases in the state sector, adoption of an import-substitution strategy of industrialization, and failure to adjust quickly to world economic conditions, especially after major oil price increases by the Organization of Petroleum Exporting Countries (OPEC). Political conflicts and wars in some of these countries also explain their poor economic development record.

Indeed, the onset of political conflict or instability in these countries may be explained mainly by the statist, interventionist economic policies their governments adopted. (See, for example, Bauer 1988.) The considerable control over economic resources such policies grant rulers raises the cost to them of losing political power through the democratic process. The tendency is to institute a one-party political system in order to assure the continued rule of those who first gained power.

Even under a one-party system, the rulers may find it expedient to retain power through bribery of potential opponents or outright repression or some combination of both. The desire on the part of some disadvantaged individuals to clean up corruption and restore the democratic political process, or merely also to gain the chance at economic and political power, may motivate frequent attempts to overthrow a ruling regime. On the part of the majority of the population in such circumstances, any change promising relief in the form of greater economic and political freedoms always seems welcome. Hence, the enthusiasm with which most coups are greeted in countries in which they occur in the Third World.

However, economic growth has been consistently positive in most middle-income countries. For the lower middle-income countries, the weighted average of annual per capita income growth between 1965 and 1986 was 2.5 percent, while those of the upper-middle-income group recorded 2.8 percent. Indeed, these growth rates are higher than the average of 2.3 percent experienced amongst industrial market economies over the same period. Among the above-average growth performers in the middle-income countries were several in Africa, including Egypt (3.1 percent), Algeria (3.5 percent), People's Republic of Congo (3.6 percent), Tunisia (3.8 percent), the Cameroon (3.9 percent), and Botswana (8.8 percent), all of which became politically independent following the Second World War. With the exception of Tunisia, whose ranking from the poorest country in the world declined from 67 in 1976 to 65, all the others improved their relative per capita income position: Egypt (36 to 53), Cameroon (38 to 59),

Congo (50 to 61), and Algeria (68 to 86). (Botswana, with a rank of 57 in 1986, was not listed in 1976.)

Per capita income growth has been even more significant among some Asian countries which became independent after the Second World War. Between 1965 and 1986 several of these countries recorded average annual growth in per capita income of 4 percent or more, including Thailand (4 percent), Malaysia (4.3 percent), Indonesia (4.6 percent), South Korea (6.7 percent), and Singapore (7.6 percent). Such growth performance significantly exceeds that of the more mature industrialized countries of Europe and North America over the same period. Only Japan's 4.3 percent growth rate comes close to the average for the group. The few middle-income countries that recorded negative average annual per capita income growth over the 20-year period but which did not fall into the category of low-income countries include El Salvador (-0.3 percent), Jamaica (-1.4 percent), and Nicaragua (-2.2 percent). (Note that El Salvador and Nicaragua have been politically independent since the early 19th century, El Salvador in 1821, and Nicaragua since 1838.)

The poor performance of these countries may be explained by their choice of state interventionist economic policies or the prevalence of political strife. El Salvador's poor performance is more accounted for by its civil strife than significant interventionist economic policies, the government having held its spending out of national income to just about 13 percent annually between 1965 and 1986. In Jamaica, the share of government spending rose from 21 percent in 1965 to 49 percent in 1980 when Manley's government was defeated, and declined slightly to 47 percent by 1985. In Nicaragua the share of government spending out of national income was only 11 percent in 1965, but it rose sharply to 30 percent in 1980, and to 56 percent in 1986.

The negative association between the share of government spending in national income and economic growth indicated by these countries is consistent with that found by Landau (1986) for a sample of 65 less developed countries (LDCs), including 22 from Africa and 11 from Asia. Similarly, Marsden (1983) finds a negative relation between the share of tax revenues to national income (GDP) and economic growth among 20 LDCs and more developed countries. Such findings should not be surprising given the fact that most of what a government spends must first be taken out of private sector incomes or savings. Even if the government borrows from abroad, some of the funds to retire the debt in future may have to be raised from taxes paid by the private sector. And because the productivity of government spending or investment is typically less than that of the private sector, the greater is the proportion of government spending in national income the less growth on average an economy would experience.

The conclusion we may draw from the above survey of the economic performance of recently independent countries is that retrogression is not a necessary consequence of political independence. Much more depends on the economic policies adopted by the government, and the degree of political tranquility fostered in the country. Indeed, the latter is very much a function of the former. It is hard to maintain political tranquility—absence of frequent attempts to change the government, often by force—while denying economic freedoms through collectivist policies (see, for example, Hayek 1944).

For Bermuda, the experiences of Jamaica, the Bahamas, and Barbados may be even more relevant since they are all island countries sharing a similar British colonial experience. Jamaica became politically independent in 1962. Ten years later, under Michael Manley, the government adopted socialist-oriented policies, including active government participation in such major industries as tourism and bauxite mining. These policies did not produce economic growth but rather an economic crisis by the late 1970s. The change of government in 1980 enabled Edward Seaga's Jamaica Labour Party (JLP) government to institute somewhat different policies, which mostly just arrested the economic decline. Whereas per capita income grew at an average annual rate of 1.9 percent between 1960 and 1976, according to World Bank estimates—Jamaica ranked 74th on the World Bank poverty scale in 1976—the growth rate between 1965 and 1986 was -1.4 percent. The ranking of per capita income also declined to 58th by 1986. In 1976 per capita income in Jamaica was (US) $1,070, but it declined to (US) $840 by 1986. The defeat of Seaga's government in February 1989 may be explained by the government's failure to significantly improve the performance of Jamaica's economy.

The Bahamas, on the other hand, has experienced continued economic growth since its independence from Britain in 1973, under the government of the Progressive Liberal Party (PLP) led by Lynden Pindling. In 1973, the earliest date for which I have data (*Financial Statistics* 1987), per capita income (gross domestic product) was (US) $3,234. By 1982, the amount more than doubled to about (US) $6,586 (see table 3). Thus, between 1973 and 1982, the average annual growth rate of per capita income in current (US) dollars was 10.6 percent.

World Bank estimates, however, show a negative average annual growth rate of 0.3 percent between 1965 and 1986. It is hard to reconcile their estimates with data from the IMF *International Financial Statistics* or earlier editions of the *World Development Report*. For example, per capita income in 1980 was given as (US) $3,790 (World Bank 1982, p. 163) and was estimated in 1986 to be (US) $7,190—hardly showing a decline.

Calculations based on data from IMF statistics show positive but less spectacular growth performance in

Table 3

Per Capita Incomes of the Bahamas, Barbados and Jamaica, Selected Years

	1974	1976	1978	1980	1982	1984
Bahamas	3,274	4,205	5,492	5,551	6,586	n.a.*
Barbados	2,815	2,823	2,939	3,443	3,086	3,335
Jamaica	1,182	1,433	1,040	1,229	1,471	827

Source: *International Financial Statistics* (1987). Estimates are current year values of gross domestic product converted to U.S. dollars.
*n.a. = not available

Barbados, another island country which became politically independent from British rule in 1966. In 1961, the country's per capita gross domestic product was about (US) $1,691. By 1985, the value had reached about (US) $3,345, having grown at an average annual rate of 3.5 percent between 1962 and 1970, 4.6 percent between 1970 and 1980, and slowed to 0.3 percent between 1980 and 1985. (World Bank 1988, p. 289, estimates per capita national income in Barbados to have grown at an average annual rate of 2.4 percent between 1965 and 1986 in constant 1980 prices.) Thus, we again find that economic retrogression following political independence is not inevitable, even for small island countries.

The above survey of the development performance of newly independent nations also suggests that race is not a relevant determinant of economic success or failure in a country. The Bahamas is about 85 percent black, and per capita income has increased under the predominantly black-led party headed by Lynden Pindling since 1967. Barbados, which is about 90 percent black, similarly has done well in terms of economic development since becoming independent in 1966. In Africa, some newly independent nations have prospered since the mid-1960s, while others have floundered. And in the Latin American basin, the economic failures of Jamaica are about matched by those of the long independent nations of El Salvador and Nicaragua whose populations are less than 10 percent black, though not predominantly white either. Finally, the poor economic performance of several Eastern European countries since the 1960s can be cited in refutation of a race theory of economic underdevelopment.

Rather, these cases show the significance of economic policy as the main determinant of failure or success. The point can be further illustrated by the diverse economic performance of contiguous countries with virtually similar peoples: East and West Germany, North and South Korea, mainland China versus Hong Kong or Taiwan, and Ghana versus Cote D'Ivoire in West Africa. In all these cases, the first mentioned country has performed poorly in economic development, especially between 1960 and 1980, while the latter countries have prospered, mainly because of different economic policy choices. Even within the same country, periods of greater economic growth often are associated with greater freedom of private enterprise. China, before and after the economic reforms of Deng Xiaoping in 1978, gives an excellent illustration of this fact. And in Ghana, positive economic growth during the years 1967 to 1971 and 1983 to 1988 is also associated with greater freedom of private enterprise compared with other periods since 1960 (Ahiakpor 1988).

Thus, the decision to become politically independent cannot meaningfully be determined on whether, by itself, independence would undermine Bermuda's economic prosperity and further development. Much more depends on the economic policies adopted after independence.

The emphasis here on economic policies may be considered too narrow for its apparent neglect of political structures. But as is becoming increasingly recognized, policies that allow greater individual economic freedom are more important for the growth of an economy than those that grant greater political freedom (see, for example, Walker 1988), although the ideal may be to have both economic and political freedoms.

Even under the current constitutional arrangements, Bermuda's economic future can be seriously harmed by the adoption of inefficient economic policies or a political ideology not conducive to efficient economic development, such as Marxism-Leninism or the pursuit of equalization of income and wealth using the coercive powers of the state (e.g., Morawetz 1980, and Jameson and Wilber 1981). An examination of Bermuda's economic structure and recent performance will help clarify these arguments.

Chapter Four

The Economy of Bermuda

The issue of greatest concern in the debate over political independence for Bermuda is the impact of such a decision on the country's economy. The main argument is that because of the structure of Bermuda's economy, which is a small, open, and services-dominated one, fears of significant policy change following independence could bring about its collapse. To evaluate these fears, we examine the structure and performance of the economy.

As mentioned above (table 1), per capita income in Bermuda is among the highest in the world. According to the country's Ministry of Finance, Bermuda ranks among "the top half-dozen countries in the world in terms of average annual income" (*Economic Review* 1988, p. 6).

Indeed, averaging the per capita income (GDP) for the two fiscal years 1985/86 and 1986/87 yields $18,000 for 1986, which is higher than the estimate of $17,225 for the U.S. according to 1987 IMF data. The World Bank estimates per capita GNP in 1986 for the U.S. to be $17,480, which is also close to the $17,409 estimate based on IMF data. (See World Bank 1988, p. 222.)

Between 1975 and 1987, Bermuda's gross domestic product per capita, measured in current prices, grew at an average annual rate of 10.6 percent while the weighted average of all prices (GDP deflator) grew at an average annual rate of 9.1 percent. The cost of living (approximated by the cost of food, accommodation, fuel and transportation, and recreation) is much higher in Bermuda than in Canada or the U.S. and has been rising faster in Bermuda than in these countries. According to IMF (1987, p. 163) estimates, the average annual growth rate of the GDP deflator between 1975 and 1985 was 7.6 percent in Canada and 6.9 percent in the U.S. However, the high per capita income in Bermuda places that country firmly among the developed countries.

Bermuda's economy is dominated by the production of services, much of which is highly skilled as is typical of many high-income countries. The labour force employed in agriculture, fishing, and quarrying since 1981 has amounted to only 1 percent annually (*Bermuda Digest of Statistics,* 1987). In comparison, the share of labour engaged in agriculture in the United Kingdom in 1980 was

3 percent (see table 4). In Canada and the U.S. the share was 5 percent and 4 percent, respectively. For all industrial market economies, the weighted average of labour force employed in agriculture in 1980 was 7 percent (World Bank 1988).

The manufacturing industry in Bermuda has employed about 3.5 percent of the labour force annually since 1981, while employment in the construction industry has averaged about 7 percent, making the total employment in "industry" about 11 percent. About 43 percent of the labour force has been employed in wholesale and retail, restaurants and hotels, and transport, storage, and communications industries. Finance and real estate services also employ about 13 percent. Another 31 percent of the labour force has been employed in activities related to "community, social, and personal services" and international bodies. Thus, in Bermuda more than 80 percent of the labour force has been employed in the service sector since 1981.

By contrast, the share of the labour force employed in non-agricultural industries (manufacturing, mining, construction, electricity, water, and gas) in Canada, Britain, and the U.S. in 1980 was 29 percent, 38 percent, and 31 percent, respectively, far higher than in Bermuda. Employment in service industries has also been lower in these countries than in Bermuda, being 65 percent in Canada, 59 percent in Britain, and 66 percent in the U.S.

Table 4

Percentage of Labour Force in Key Sectors, Selected Countries

	Agriculture		*Industry*		*Services*	
	1965	*1980*	*1965*	*1980*	*1965*	*1980*
Jamaica	37	31	20	16	43	52
Hong Kong	6	2	53	51	41	47
Canada	10	5	33	29	57	65
United States	5	4	35	31	60	66
United Kingdom	3	3	47	38	50	59
Trinidad and Tobago	20	10	35	39	45	51

Source: World Bank (1988), table 31.

Also, note some of the similarities in the structure of employment between Bermuda, Honk Kong, Jamaica, and Trinidad and Tobago. Employment in agriculture has declined significantly in Hong Kong (to 2 percent in 1980) while service sector employment has increased from 41 percent to 47 percent. In Jamaica, service sector employment has increased from 43 percent to 52 percent; and in Trinidad and Tobago, from 45 percent to 51 percent. But per capita incomes are far less in these countries than in Bermuda.

Apart from its dependence on the production of services, Bermuda's economy is also significantly dependent on foreign demand. Such dependence may be due in part to the small size of the island, forcing a greater degree of specialization in economic activity. Until the passage of restrictive tariffs (Smoot-Hawley Act) in the U.S. which virtually eliminated the market for Bermuda's export of agricultural produce (fresh vegetables) during the late 1920s, such exports had been the basis of economic growth for the country since the late 19th century. Until the late 1800s, ship building and salt exports were the country's main economic activities.

Dependence on foreign demand for increased wealth creation is thus not new to Bermuda, neither is it necessarily detrimental to an economy. In 1986 the export of goods and non-factor services amounted to more than 60 percent of gross domestic product in countries that also were among the fastest growing economies in the world, including Botswana (63 percent), Belgium (69 percent), and Hong Kong (112 percent). (See World Bank 1988, and table 5.) And between 1965 and 1986, the average annual growth rate of per capita national income in constant 1980 (US) dollars was 8.8 percent for Botswana, 2.7 percent for Belgium, and 6.2 percent for Hong Kong. In the Bahamas, tourism alone is estimated to have accounted for some 60 percent of the national income in 1987 (see the Maldon Institute 1988) but, as noted above, the Bahamas economy has performed quite well over the last two decades or so.

Since the 1970s, more than 60 percent of Bermuda's gross domestic product (GDP) has been composed of goods and services sold to foreigners (see *Bermuda Digest of Statistics* 1987, p. 78). In 1975/76 the proportion stood at 62 percent and increased to 67 percent in 1980/81 before declining to 63 percent in 1985/86. Expenditures by visitors to Bermuda constitute the most significant of foreign-related sales. Until 1984/85 such expenditures amounted to more than 50 percent of Bermuda's export revenue, but they fell to 49 percent by 1985/86. Although the nominal dollar amount of visitor expenditures has been on the decline since 1977/78, increases in the value of "other goods and services" and international company expenditures also account for the relative decline in the share of visitor expenditures in total exports. Expenditures by foreign companies, which are the second most important of export items, have been on the increase from 23 percent of receipts in 1978/79 to 29 percent in 1985/86 after having peaked at 32 percent in 1981/82.

Table 5
Exports of Goods and Non-factor Services as Share of GDP, Selected Countries

	1975	1978	1981	1983	1985
Bahamas	79.9	75.5	94.2	n.a.*	n.a.*
Barbados	54.0	57.5	56.3	64.5	62.4
Belgium	46.5	50.3	64.0	70.6	73.3
Botswana	60.0	62.9	53.5	79.7	100.1
Hong Kong	64.0	66.3	73.9	76.8	90.0
Jamaica	36.7	42.1	47.4	34.2	57.8
Netherlands	47.4	42.3	55.9	54.9	61.9
Singapore	140.0	169.7	203.9	172.2	n.a.*
Switzerland	77.7	62.4	70.0	61.6	n.a.*
Trinidad and Tobago	52.0	44.8	45.1	n.a.*	n.a.*

Source: *International Financial Statistics: Supplement on Trade Statistics* (1988).
*n.a. = not available

The twin main features of the Bermudian economy—services and foreign-oriented production—have led some to predict dire consequences if foreign firms and governments, such as the U.S. and Canada, should close down their activities following political independence. The Archer Report (1987), though not directly focused on the question of political independence, contains some frightening estimates of the number of jobs and the income that would be lost if foreign companies were to leave and the U.S. and Canadian military installations were closed down.

The argument is developed along the following lines. Much of the installed productive capacity in Bermuda, mainly offices, hotels, and restaurants, are intended to service foreign demand. A collapse of foreign confidence in Bermuda would mean laying off many workers employed in such facilities. An economy based on the production of real goods such as cocoa, coffee, manufactures, or minerals might be able to continue with such activities (even if on a reduced scale) in anticipation of finding alternative markets while current output is stored. But lay-offs in service industries in response to significant contraction in demand would be quicker and more significant.

However, this argument is questionable on several grounds. Perhaps the most important one is whether the constitutional status of a country matters much in the decision of foreign firms to invest there. Similarly, does the constitutional status of a country significantly affect its ability to attract tourists? And are service-dominated economies more prone to income fluctuations than real goods production economies?

None of these questions warrants an affirmative answer, either on the basis of the evidence or in principle. Numerous countries have become politically independent since the Second World War. And although most foreign direct investment in the world still takes place among the industrial market economies, there has been a substantial increase in the volume of foreign investment going to newly independent countries, especially since the 1960s.

The remarkable economic success of such countries as Singapore, South Korea, and Taiwan during the 1970s—all countries which became politically independent after the Second World War—is to a large extent explained by the presence of foreign capital. (See, for example, Stoever 1986, for a detailed discussion of South Korea's path to economic development since the 1960s.) Of course, a congenial domestic policy environment (including political stability) also has made this possible.

Similarly, within the Caribbean basin further to the south of Bermuda, foreign investment has continued despite these countries having attained political independence, mostly since the 1960s. Thus, a study of the Bahamas concludes that "confidence in the essential stability of the [country] is widespread" (The Maldon

Institute 1988, p. 10). The study backs up this conclusion by noting the presence of nearly 300 international banks from 27 countries, among which are "Bank America International New York, Bankers Trust Co., Morgan Guarantee Trust Co., Citizens and Southern Corp., Citibank, The Chase Manhattan Bank, N.A., First National Bank of Boston, Lloyds Bank International, Royal Bank of Canada, and Swiss Bank Corp."

That foreign investment (in real productive or financial assets) has continued in many of these newly independent countries despite their changed constitutional status should not be surprising. The primary purpose of any firm's investment is to make profits. The need to earn high enough profits to pay an attractive rate of return on investment is probably greater for firms operating in a foreign environment. Investors or shareholders in such companies may need to be induced with a higher return to assume the additional risks associated with the firm's operations in a foreign country. There are usually competing investment opportunities at home where investors may feel more secure about their investments. Thus, unless political instability threatens the profitability of firms, they are not likely to be dissuaded from investing in a country because of its constitutional status.

Indeed, capital appears to be blind to constitutional or, sometimes, moral or ideological differences between investors and the people of countries in which they invest. This is why capital from western democracies continues to be invested in communist countries as well as in racist states such as South Africa, although some investors may publicly denounce the behaviour of rulers in those countries toward their citizens.

The absence of corporate income tax as well as taxes on capital gains in Bermuda, more than any other reason, may significantly explain the relatively large number of foreign firms in the country, many of which have a minimal physical presence. It is hardly out of benevolence toward or a special liking for the people of Bermuda that a large number of foreign firms have located on the island. Unless the economic incentives for their being registered or physically located in Bermuda change following the attainment of political independence, there is little reason why the flow of foreign investment to Bermuda should be reversed if the people opt for political independence.

The fear of vulnerability to economic disaster due to Bermuda's significant reliance on the exportation of services may derive from the common sense argument that those who put all their eggs in one basket stand to suffer significant losses when things go wrong. Such thinking also has led some to advise that countries diversify their economies, a sort of portfolio risk minimizing approach to country investment. However, it can be shown that the dangers of product specialization differ according to product type and the significance of a country's output in total world supply.

The product type argument has recently been demonstrated by Mullor-Sebastian (1988). Although the argument has been illustrated for real goods, it can be applied to services such as tourism. Simply stated, it is that "export instability is related to comparative advantage in such a manner that a country experiences relatively less instability in export earnings of a product when it has a comparative advantage in that product" (p. 218). And an important determinant of such an advantage is the country's comparative level of development or skill in the production and marketing of the product. These factors affect both the quality and cost of products and influence consumers' choice in the competitive world market. Thus, more experienced and cost-effective tourist enterprises may be less affected by fluctuations in tourist demands than less experienced and more costly operators.

Another relevant factor in considering the possible consequences of changes in foreign demand for services exported from Bermuda, particularly tourism, is the fact that the country is one among many from which such services may be bought in the world. Thus, variations in the demand for tourist services owing to economic recession in major source countries, for example, would be distributed among competing suppliers. For tourists, location, facilities they can use, historical interest of a place, the attitude of local people toward tourists, and the cost of the visit are among the most important determinants of choosing where to go. To a certain degree, some of these attributes may be peculiar to a place, but few locations lack any competition in another country. For example, the "friendliness and hospitality of Bermudians, cleanliness and peacefulness of the islands as well as scenic beauty" are cited as the most consistent reasons tourists have given for visiting Bermuda (*Bermuda Report: 1980-1984,* p. 92). But some of these attributes could well be cited for many island tourist spots in the world, including Cuba, the Bahamas, Barbados, or Hawaii. Thus Stryker McGuire (1989, p. 37) observes that Cuba's "pristine beaches are a match for those at other, far more expensive Caribbean sites." Others describe the Bahamas as a "tourist mecca" (The Maldon Institute 1988, p. 1). Nevertheless, some features of Bermuda which derive from its history and geography are unique to the island. Marketing these features, and tourists' preferences for them, would thus determine by how much the country's economy may be affected by changes in world tourism demand.

What should be of more relevant concern for the tourism industry in Bermuda is its increasing regulation by government, not the consequences of political independence. According to the *Bermuda Report,* government regulation of the industry has increased significantly since 1968, particularly in limiting accommodation capacity within the industry and the number of tour arrivals. Thus, under the Hotels Act (1969), "A moratorium was placed on the construction of new hotels while expansion of existing hotel properties was limited."

It requires a much more detailed study than this to make definitive conclusions about the consequences of implementing this act. But it is well-known that hotel accommodation in Bermuda is very expensive compared to similar facilities in Canada, the U.S., or some other tourist destinations in the Caribbean. Some may want to explain away the negative impact of the resulting high costs to tourists for the industry by arguing that it is quality tourists (and high spenders) the government wants to attract. But it is also true that the flow of tourists to Bermuda has declined somewhat, especially since 1980, and the number of days spent has also declined. However, total earnings from tourism has continued to grow, although not significantly; about 6 percent per year since 1980. (See *Economic Review* 1988, p. 14.) These trends seem to underlie Eldon Trimingham's forceful comments on tourism policy: "The most serious misconception [is] that we could fill our hotels despite the prices... Our problem is we charge...Rolls Royce prices and deliver, at best, a Buick" (Speech to the Hamilton Rotary, August 1988). This is why greater government regulation of the industry may be a greater threat to its growth and profitability than political independence.

In summary, Bermuda's economic structure is similar in many respects to that of other high-income countries. Dependence on foreign demand has not been a significant hindrance to the country's economic growth in the past. There is little reason to expect the resilience of the economy, which reflects the enterprise of its people, to change after the attainment of political independence. What must be a relevant concern, however, is the cost of political independence in terms of additional resources required to provide those services Bermudians now enjoy from being a dependent colony weighed against the expected benefits of independence. To that discussion we now turn.

Chapter Five

Estimating the Costs and Benefits of Political Independence

How much political independence would cost is one of the most frequently asked questions in the independence debate. But the persistence of this question also testifies to the fact that no one can put definite amounts on the direct cost of independence. The most one can do is postulate a range of values based on different assumptions about the form governance as well as international representation of the country would take after political independence. Furthermore, such an attempt at estimating costs requires specialized skills in judging the adequacy of a country's representation and its defence requirements. Even in possession of such skills, an analyst requires an enormous amount of information on components of costs in delivering the required services. I confess to being unskilled in designing adequate international representation or national security. However, on the assumption that previous official attempts to estimate some of these costs embody the considered views of experts, I base my discussion on them. I also draw on comparable evidence from other countries.

As pointed out in government documents on the subject, the most evident additional costs to Bermudians on becoming politically independent are those of external representation and national defence. Under the present constitutional arrangements, the government of Bermuda takes charge of administering the economy and running social services. The British government, through the Governor, controls external affairs and national security—the police force and the Bermuda regiment. Thus, although the government of Bermuda operates trade offices in Britain, Canada, and the U.S., British consular services across the world provide protection to citizens of Bermuda. Britain also represents the interests of Bermuda in international negotiations, to which representatives of Bermuda are usually invited to attend. Political independence relieves the British government of the obligation to provide these services to Bermuda.

In estimating the cost of foreign representation, previous attempts have considered three options: (a) establishing no diplomatic missions, (b) upgrading existing Department of Tourism Offices in London, Toronto, and

New York to the status of diplomatic missions, and (c) establishing small diplomatic missions in London, Ottawa, and Washington in addition to the tourism offices. The first option involves relying on help from the missions of Britain and other countries, "supplemented by direct correspondence, ministerial visits, and the appointment of part-time agents or Honorary Consuls in London, Ottawa and Washington" (*Independence for Bermuda* 1977, p. 27). There also would be no membership in international agencies, such as the IMF and the World Bank, except subscriptions to specialized agencies of the United Nations Organization (UN) and the Commonwealth Secretariat.

Using June 1977 values, the first option was expected to cost $577,000. The second option, involving similar international relations, was estimated to cost $767,000. Estimated cost of the third option, which includes full membership of international agencies, was $1,307,000. The additional cost of providing enhanced national security (both police and military) was estimated at $600,000.

In total, the additional direct cost of independence amounts to $1,177,000 under option 1, $1,367,000 under option 2, and $1,907,000 under option 3, in 1977 dollars. However, the defence expenditure component of the costs was expected to decrease by $500,000 after the first year. Thus, abstracting from inflation, the subsequent additional cost of independence was expected to be $677,000 under option 1, $867,000 under option 2, and $1,407,000 under option 3.

With a population of 54,302 in 1977, the additional cost of independence that year would have amounted to $21.68 per person under option 1, $25.17 under option 2, and $35.12 under option 3. Needless to say, the costs are significantly higher per working person, who presumably bears most of the expense. Because the average ratio of labour force to population is about 57 percent (*Bermuda Digest of Statistics* 1987), these values have to be multiplied by a factor of 1.75 to obtain the costs per worker. They become $37.94 under option 1, $44.05 under option 2, and $61.46 under option 3.

Between 1976 and 1987 the average of all prices (GDP deflator) rose at an average annual rate of 9.1 percent (*Bermuda: An Economic Review* 1988, p. 12; retail prices increased by a smaller rate, 7.3 percent). Applying this rate of price increase to the additional (direct) costs of independence would increase the values in 1986 to $2,577,630 for option 1, $2,993,730 for option 2, and $4,176,330 for option 3. In terms of per capita expenditure, the values amount to $44.74 under option 1, $51.96 under option 2, and $72.48 under option 3, or $78.30, $90.93, and $126.84 per adult working population, respectively.

It is legitimate to ask how realistic are these figures. Again, this is a difficult question to answer definitively. Their accuracy also depends on the goals the dollar values are supposed to attain. For example, the estimated cost of services provided to Bermuda by the U.S. Naval Station alone in 1985 was $8.8 million (Archer 1987), which is more than twice the total additional direct cost of independence projected into 1986 prices. On the other hand, comparison of the additional defence costs with the total amounts spent in Barbados, Jamaica, Trinidad and Tobago introduces a greater sense of accuracy for the estimated costs (see table 6).

Projecting the defence estimates of 1977 to 1980 by the average annual growth rate of the GDP deflator amounts to $779,400 or $14.20 per capita. This is higher than the per capita defence expenditures of Barbados ($7), Jamaica ($9), and Trinidad and Tobago ($13) in 1980. But, these countries also have larger populations and more land than Bermuda. For example, the total defence expenditure of Barbados in 1980 was $2 million, and that of Jamaica, $20 million. Their populations were estimated at 250,000, and 2.17 million, respectively (*International Financial Statistics: Yearbook* 1987), compared with 54,870 for Bermuda in 1980. While Bermuda covers 53 square kilometres of land, Barbados covers 430 square kilometres, and Jamaica, 11,000 square kilometres (Trinidad and Tobago has 5,000 square kilometres). Thus, these countries may be experiencing economies of scale in defence expenditures. On the other hand, the $8.8 million operating costs of the U.S. Naval Station in 1985 appear excessive for Bermuda's security needs.

Also note that the estimated additional recurrent expenditure would have amounted to $129,860 or only $2.37 per capita in 1980. Such a low estimate is premised

Table 6

Per Capita Income and Defence Expenditures, Selected Countries (US$)

	1980		1983	
	Income	Defence	Income	Defence
Barbados	3,443	7	4,202	36
Jamaica	1,229	9	926	n.a.*
Trinidad and Tobago	5,843	13	6,474	n.a.*
Canada	10,826	174	13,095	255
United Kingdom	9,818	342	7,746	n.a.*
United States	11,787	555	14,521	851

Note: Per capita income (GDP) values are based on data from *International Financial Statistics* (1987), 1980 defence estimates obtained from Kurian (1984), and 1983 defence estimates obtained from *Statistical Yearbook* (1988).

*n.a. = not available

on the fact that "there are no neighbouring countries near enough [to Bermuda] to pose problems over international boundaries or illegal immigration" (*Independence for Bermuda* 1987, p. 12). The estimates also have remained unchallenged, probably on the grounds that past deficiencies in the Security Services "have been largely eliminated and overall the internal security capabilities have been considerably enhanced" (*Independence for Bermuda,* p. 16).

A complete evaluation of the estimates cannot be made unless we know the total expenditures on national security in Bermuda while still a dependent territory. But it would be unreasonable to dispute the conclusions of three previous studies regarding the cost of defence for independent Bermuda in the absence of persuasive reasons for doing so.

Whatever the true costs, another question to consider is whether Bermudians can afford the additional costs of independence. On the basis of experiences elsewhere, the answer to that question must be yes. Consider, for example, the defence expenditures (military alone) in some countries with similar per capita incomes as Bermuda's. Such expenditures in 1980 were $174 in Canada, $342 in Britain, and $555 in the U.S. The argument can be made that if people in these countries can afford the costs of being politically independent, so can the people of Bermuda. However, the wisdom of incurring any expenditure does not lie in the purchasing power of the spender. Rather, it depends on what one gets in return compared to what else one could have spent the money on. Pursuit of that evaluation leads to the question: what are the anticipated benefits of political independence for Bermuda?

This is a question to which different people would have different answers. The intensity with which different people assign values to the anticipated benefits would typically not be the same. In spite of these difficulties in deriving unique, generally acceptable conclusions, an assessment of some often mentioned benefits of political independence for Bermuda may be helpful in making an informed decision. They include:

>(a) the ability of the Bermudian government to control the security forces,

>(b) the government's freedom to decide the nature of Bermuda's external relations, and

>(c) fostering a greater sense of Bermudian identity.

(Obviously, others can be cited for examination, e.g., enhancement of self-worth as claimed by some nationalists. But the above were mentioned most frequently by those I talked with during my interviews.)

It is hard to find significant benefits for Bermudians on the first of these grounds. The present constitutional arrangements have performed quite well in maintaining national security as well as law and order. Bermuda has enjoyed external protection from Britain, Canada, and the U.S. in exchange for the use of Bermudian territory by the latter two. Similar arrangements may continue after independence (and past government reports have indicated their desirability) as has happened in other countries.

For example, because U.S. Naval and Air Force facilities are located in the Bahamas, that country could count on U.S. assistance against external aggression, should that arise. But the Bahamas also spends a considerable amount on national security ($60 million or about $251 per capita in 1987, mostly because of a special anti-drug campaign) because it is a sovereign nation. Internally, Bermudians have shown little anxiety over security, according to Gurr's (1984) survey findings. Thus, unless the present arrangements can be shown to have worked poorly in promoting law and order, the benefits of political independence appear small in this regard.

A nationalist may respond by arguing that the inability to find significant benefits is not a good reason a foreign government should exercise control over the security arrangements of another country. Yet some political leaders eager for Bermuda to attain independence also have expressed reservations about power over the security forces being transferred to the current Premier. However, they themselves would not hesitate to exercise such powers. Such arguments appear to suggest that whatever the gains from Bermudian control of the security forces may be, they are not substantial enough to outweigh suspicions, perhaps petty, among current political leaders.

Associated with the above sentiment may be a nationalist's dislike of a Briton rather than a Bermudian being appointed Governor of the island. To them the presence of a foreigner with reserved powers in the governance of another country connotes some degree of subjugation. This is why they might prefer a different constitutional arrangement, e.g., associated statehood, whereby Bermudians would appoint their own (Bermudian) Governor while the head of state continues to be the British monarch. In the first place, such an arrangement has been ruled out of the options available to Bermuda. But were that possible, it is unlikely that suspicion over the constitutional neutrality of the person holding such a position would be absent. Thus, whether it is control over the security forces or appointment of a Bermudian Governor, there do not as yet appear to be large gains for the general public.

Those who anticipate greater benefits to Bermuda from managing the country's external relations directly have pointed to a greater ability of the government to negotiate aviation and naval treaties better suited to the interests of Bermuda. The argument suggests that negotiations through the British government have not been satisfactory. If so, it has to be shown that negotiating as a small country would yield greater benefits than doing so through a nation with significant world stature, or that the existing negotiating process cannot be improved upon. Of course, in this modern age where "gun-boat" diplomacy frequently is no longer a preferred option for big, powerful nations, a small country on its own can successfully extract large gains in international negotiations. But few would be content with merely the prospect of that happening instead of a more concrete demonstration of the chances of such success.

It also may be conceded that representation of one's interests by others does not always reflect one's true feelings. This fact is underscored by those who point to what they consider to be an awkward situation for the government of Bermuda being unable to impose trade sanctions on South Africa as governments of several other Commonwealth countries have done, at least in official proclamations. (Bermuda's present position is dictated by that of Britain.) Yet, unless the symbolism of sanctions matters more than its substance to those who make the point, the inability of Bermuda's government to impose sanctions is not that serious.

The true effect of trade sanctions, which is to deny a market to the products of the country upon which they are imposed, also can be achieved by Bermudians (and people in other countries) individually refusing to buy goods made in South Africa. Of course, the effect of such individual action may fall far short of nationally-mandated sanctions if those who care enough about the issue are in a small minority. But even if the government of Bermuda were to have imposed sanctions, the fact that Bermuda's market is of little significance to South African exports means sanctions would have little material effect on the economy of South Africa. Thus there also does not seem to be much tangible gain from independence on this score.

Note that I do not here deny the loss of an option to the government of Bermuda from its being a dependent colony. However, my argument relates to the ultimate significance of such a loss. Indeed, careful consideration of the Bermuda government's situation helps us appreciate another dimension of government-mandated actions, such as a trade sanction. Often they are means by which some members of society impose their preferences or sense of morality on others, even where the contrary preferences inflict no injury on them. Yet where the preferences of the many differ strongly from the choices mandated by government, the main result is large-scale breaking of laws or regulations, e.g., in-smuggling of goods without significant effects on the economy of the country targeted with trade sanctions.

Perhaps if the sanctions issue had been viewed in this light, many governments would have sought a dialogue with their citizens in an attempt to persuade rather than trying, with considerable difficulty, to force compliance out of them. If most individuals believed the ends to be realized from boycotting South African goods were worth more than their gains from purchasing them, there would have been little need to seek world-wide government-imposed trade sanctions. Importers of such goods would find little market for them, make losses, and refrain from further importation. Similarly, numerous workers from other African countries might not be trekking into South Africa for work, many illegally, to the embarrassment of their national governments if enough of them felt the incomes they received from working in South Africa were not worth the indignity of being employed there.

It is a somewhat different question whether there are net benefits to Bermudians from having ships registered under the Bermuda flag rather than operating under British naval laws (The United Kingdom Merchant Shipping Act, 1894). On one hand, Bermuda would gain greater control over regulation of shipping following independence. But, on the other hand, fewer ships may want to be registered under the Bermuda flag once British consular protection is lost. Once again the net benefits are not clear.

It also seems doubtful that attainment of political independence would necessarily foster a greater sense of Bermudianness in the country. Many now cherish being Bermudians first, and having the quasi-British nationality associated with it. They seem to enjoy some benefit from the international recognition and protection that status provides. Such people might feel a sense of loss with political independence. Similarly, foreign-born Bermudians also may have to choose between the nationality of their birth and that of Bermuda. But even those who choose the latter may never feel completely

"Bermudian." It is just not that easy to give up feelings for one's birthplace.

However, a country in which people do not feel secure or have the freedom to pursue development of their potential, including creation of wealth, is not likely to engender a strong sense of belonging among its nationals. The exodus of people from places that are politically independent but where insecurity of individuals, political instability, and economic deprivations abound may be cited in illustration of this fact.

Britain, Canada, France, West Germany, and the U.S., on the other hand, have become the main recipients of such an exodus because their governments are able to ensure security and freedom for individuals, which in turn have promoted political stability and economic development. But Bermudians, black or white, seem quite happy with their lives on the island (Gurr 1984). Particularly among blacks I talked with, I have never heard a people speak with so much inclusiveness as indicated by their use of the pronoun "we." Furthermore, in the 1984 survey by Gurr, 72 percent of those interviewed thought life in Bermuda was better than in Britain, Canada, or the U.S., while 80 percent thought they were better off than those in the Caribbean islands. Thus, unless an important reason for choosing independence is to get rid of some foreign-born Bermudians who might not want to give up legal allegiance to their country of birth, it is hard to claim substantial benefits on the grounds of fostering greater

Bermudianness. They probably already feel as Bermudian as they ever would or could.

And what about the proposition that political independence is for blacks the logical progression from emancipation? First, I found little evidence that many blacks feel this way. Indeed, many would rather not be reminded of their slave past; not because they wish to deny it, but rather because they find it quite irrelevant to their lives now. Of course, many blacks recognize forms of racial prejudice in Bermuda from non-blacks (Gurr 1984). But being among the most travelled people in the world, Bermudian blacks also recognize the existence of racial prejudice in many other countries, including those in which blacks constitute a majority of the population. Thus, unless the practice of racial prejudice were institutionalized, and therefore remediable through legal and political actions as was the case in the 1950s and 1960s, there would seem to be little to gain from seeking political independence in order to pursue a mainly black agenda. To a considerable degree, the formation and activities of the United Bermuda Party seem to have rendered a black agenda almost an irrelevant political cause in Bermuda.

The argument that being a colony has conferred the benefits of economic growth on Bermuda, or its corollary which suggests that becoming independent would undermine economic prosperity in the country, already has been dealt with above (chapters 3 and 4). There is little validity to either of its versions. Thus, the main conclusion suggested by the discussion in this chapter is that Bermudians can afford the expense of becoming politically independent. However, the anticipated benefits of independence do not now appear to be worth the costs.

Chapter Six

What Choice, and When?

The fact that Bermuda still remains a colony of Britain,
although the independence question has been debated
actively since its introduction in parliament in 1977, may
be interpreted to mean a vote by the people against
independence. The United Bermuda Party government has
not pushed the matter to a vote because, from its own
reading of the public mood, the people are against it. Thus,
Premier John Swan in September 1988 suspended active
discussion of the independence question with two
sentences:

> *I know that the recent focus on
> Independence has caused some anxiety in
> certain sectors of the community. As*

Premier, I respect your desire to close this chapter for the time being (The Royal Gazette, September 28, p. 2).

As far as the British Crown is concerned, Bermuda will become independent when the majority of the population so desires. But Britain would not unilaterally abandon its constitutional role as Bermuda's "protector." Ironic as it may seem then, it is Britain that really may determine whether Bermudians choose soon to become independent or continue with the status quo.

Independence will come about when most people estimate the costs of remaining a dependent colony to be greater than the benefits. Such an estimation could result from actions of the British government, through the Governor, which frustrate some popular aspirations of Bermudians. The actions may be those affecting the economic, political, or social dimensions of life in Bermuda.

It is hard to construct a reasonable scenario of the kinds of things that might change the benefit/cost calculations of Bermudians in favour of independence. But suppose under the reserved powers of the Governor, which include disregarding advice of the governor's council, some internal security measures are taken which offend the majority of Bermudians. Clearly such an action would raise the value of independence by making it the easiest legal way to change an intolerable situation. Similarly, should

68

Britain adopt racially intolerable policies at home, a move which would attract world condemnation, many Bermudians whether black or white might want to show their condemnation of such a policy by dissociating themselves with the British Crown. But so long as Britain remains a country of decency and civility, and the Governor performs his duties in harmonious consultation with the Premier and other members of the governor's council, the expected benefits of political independence likely would continue to be estimated as less than, or at most equal to, the costs. Under such circumstances, the option for independence will continue to be rejected, and justifiably so. The odds also seem loaded against choosing independence under the present circumstances because the choice once made is practically irreversible.

The independence dilemma also appears complicated for many in Bermuda because their immediate concerns are not those that require command over external relations or national defence to solve. They are mainly economic, including housing and the general high cost of living. Surprisingly, I found several people, including supporters of the ruling and opposition parties, who think affluence is one of the country's problems! Perhaps those who make this claim have something else in mind than "affluence," for surely they would like to have higher real incomes and wealth than they now have, which is why they also complain about the high cost of living in Bermuda. Many in Bermuda also work at more than one job in order to make ends meet, that is, to enjoy a higher standard of living than would be possible on the salary from one job. Some refer to this phenomenon as "over-employment" in Bermuda, and wish there were some unemployment to "cool off" the economy. But of course, those who argue this way hardly want to be the ones unemployed. Thus, they well may have some other genuine argument in mind which I fail to understand because of their choice of words.

Most if not all of Bermuda's economic problems can be solved within the constitutional powers of the government, and many people believe this. For example, removing the ceiling on interest rates as part of a programme to liberalize the financial markets and restraining the growth of money supply (currency) would both curb inflation and ease the pressure on house prices. (Official thinking still does not seem to recognize currency inflation as the basic source of price inflation in Bermuda. See, for example, the *Economic Review* 1988.) Similarly, facing up to the fact that building upwards is the inevitable way of the future in Bermuda, rather than continuing to impose height restrictions, would ease the cost of dwelling places. And if there is excess demand for labour pushing up wage costs, easing the current stringent restrictions on immigration or hiring foreign labour would help solve the problem. Thus, in the face of readily solvable economic problems, some are likely to interpret pursuit of independence as an attempt by the government to divert attention from its weakness in dealing with them. But, for all we know, such reading of the matter may be quite mistaken.

It would be inappropriate to dismiss the possibility of political independence for Bermuda at any time in the future. Nothing discussed in this study warrants such a conclusion. There is also no serious reason to expect that the kinds of political, social, and economic institutions that have enabled people in Bermuda, both black and white, to prosper over the decades would suddenly crumble after political independence. Moreover, the people are sufficiently affluent to bear quite easily the direct costs of the new constitutional status, if they so choose.

Meanwhile, the challenge for advocates of independence is to convince the majority that (a) they bear some inordinate burden (including a diminution of their self-worth) for choosing to be a dependent colony, or (b) there are significant benefits (over the costs) to be derived from the change of status. Until they can accomplish either of these two tasks, the bet must be that Bermuda will continue to remain somewhat an enigma to many in other countries: a people—predominantly black—who choose a colonial status with Britain while denunciations of colonialism and neocolonialism continue to be heard in many parts of the world. (Of course, there are other examples of people choosing not to be politically independent, e.g., Puerto Rico's status with the U.S. However, there are some peculiarities in the Bermuda experience which are not comparable to these others.)

The fact of the matter is that Bermuda's present status gives the people a security umbrella under which they can pursue their domestic agenda in an environment of considerable social and political freedom and stability. Unlike many other countries where political independence was expected to open the door to economic prosperity or development, Bermuda already is one of the most prosperous countries in the world, with a higher per capita income than the "mother" country. In turning down political independence, therefore, Bermudians appear to be saying they would rather not spend money for a status from which they do not expect to gain much in return. Given the history of colonial peoples since the Second World War and Bermuda's own social history, it must take a bit of courage and realism for the majority of Bermudians to say this.

References

Ahiakpor, James C.W., "Creating the Structures for a Dynamic and Efficient Economy: The Case of Ghana." In Bodo B. Gemper, ed., *The International Trend Towards Indicative Targeting*. Hamburg: Verlag Weltarchiv GmbH, 1988, pp. 189-202.

Bauer, Peter T., "Black Africa: Free or Oppressed?" In Michael Walker (ed.), *Freedom, Democracy, and Economic Welfare. Vancouver, B.C.: The Fraser Institute, 1988, pp. 213-23*.

Archer, Brian, *The Bermudian Economy: An Impact Study*. Hamilton, Bermuda: Ministry of Finance, 1987.

Duignan, Peter and Jackson, Robert H., *Politics & Government in African States: 1960-1985*. London: Croom Helm and Stanford: Hoover Institution Press, 1986.

Government of Bermuda, *Bermuda Digest of Statistics*. Hamilton, Bermuda: Ministry of Finance, 1987.

Government of Bermuda, *Bermuda Report: 1980-1984*. Hamilton, Bermuda: Department of Public Relations (n.d.).

Government of Bermuda, *Bermuda: An Economic Review*. Hamilton, Bermuda: Ministry of Finance, 1988.

Government of Bermuda, *Independence for Bermuda: A Discussion Paper*. Hamilton, Bermuda: The Cabinet Office, 1977.

Government of Bermuda, *Independence for Bermuda: A Compilation of Official Documents*. Hamilton, Bermuda, 1987.

Gurr, Ted Robert, *The Quality of Life and Prospects for Change in Bermuda*. Hamilton, Bermuda: Government of Bermuda, 1984.

Hayek, Friedrich A., *The Road to Serfdom*. Chicago: University of Chicago Press, 1944.

International Monetary Fund, *International Financial Statistics: Yearbook*. Washington, D.C., 1987.

_____, *International Financial Statistics: Supplement on Trade Statistics*. Washington, D.C., 1988.

Jameson, Kenneth P. and Wilber, Charles K., "Socialism and Development: Editors' Introduction." *World Development,* 9 (September/October 1981), pp. 803-11.

Kurian, George T., *The New Book of World Rankings*. New York: Facts on File, 1984.

Landau, Daniel, "Government and Economic Growth in the Less Developed Countries: An Empirical Study for 1960-1980," *Economic Development and Cultural Change*. 35 (October 1986), pp. 35-75.

Maldon Institute, The, *The Bahamas: A Political Risk Analysis*. Washington, D.C., 1988.

Marsden, Keith, "Links Between Taxes and Economic Growth," *Staff Working Paper*. No. 605, The World Bank, Washington, D.C., 1983.

Marshall, Alfred, *Principles of Economics*. 8th ed., London: Macmillan, 1964.

McGuire, Stryker, "White Sand, Blue Seas—And Big Dreams," *Newsweek,* 9 January, 1989, p. 37.

Morawetz, David, "Economic Lessons from Some Small Socialist Developing Countries." *World Development,* 8 (May/June 1980), pp. 337-69.

Mullor-Sebastian, Alicia, "A New Approach to the Relation Between Export Instability and Economic Development." *Economic Development and Cultural Change,* 36 (January 1988), pp. 217-36.

Musson, Nellie E., *Mind the Onion Seed*. Hamilton, Bermuda: Musson's, 1979.

Nkrumah, Kwame, *Ghana: The Autobiography of Kwame Nkrumah*. London: Nelson, 1959.

_____, *Africa Must Unite*. New York: International Publishers, 1963.

Packwood, Cyril O., *Chained on the Rock*. New York: Torres, 1975.

75

Royal Gazette, The. Hamilton, Bermuda, 15 June & 28 September 1988.

Smith, James E., *Slavery in Bermuda*. New York: Vantage, 1976.

Stoever, William A., "Foreign Investment as an Aid in Moving from Least Developed to Newly Industrializing: A Study in Korea." *Journal of Developing Areas,* 20 (January 1986), pp. 223-48.

Trimingham, Eldon, "Speech given to the Hamilton Rotary." 23 August 1988.

Walker, Michael A., ed., *Freedom, Democracy, and Economic Welfare*. Vancouver, B.C.: The Fraser Institute, 1988.

World Bank, The. *World Development Report 1982*. New York: Oxford University Press, 1982.

_____, *World Development Report 1988*. New York: Oxford University Press, 1988.